C. P. Kumar

The Path to Peace: Overcoming Corruption, Violence, and Hatred in Our World

The Path to Peace: Overcoming Corruption, Violence, and Hatred in Our World

C. P. Kumar

Reiki Healer

Roorkee - 247667, India

Copyright © 2023 C. P. Kumar

All rights reserved.

DEDICATION

To all the individuals and organizations who work tirelessly towards promoting peace, fighting corruption, and overcoming violence and hatred, this book is dedicated to you. Your unwavering commitment to creating a better world inspires us all to join hands and work towards a future free of conflict and strife. May your efforts be rewarded with a world that is more just, equitable, and peaceful, where all individuals are able to thrive and live in harmony.

C. P. Kumar

CONTENTS

PREFACE

The world we live in today is marked by conflict, corruption, and violence. The quest for peace remains an elusive one, yet it remains a fundamental human aspiration. This book, "The Path to Peace: Overcoming Corruption, Violence, and Hatred in Our World," explores the multifaceted dimensions of peace and provides a roadmap for individuals and communities seeking to create a more peaceful world.

The book is divided into sixteen chapters that address various aspects of peacebuilding. The chapters cover topics such as the importance of peace, the roots of corruption, the role of education in overcoming corruption, the various forms of violence, and the importance of empathy and dialogue in promoting peace.

The book also explores the challenges that arise when working towards peace, including political, economic, and social factors. It proposes solutions for overcoming these challenges and fostering a culture of peace.

Drawing on examples from around the world, the book presents a comprehensive overview of the challenges we face in achieving peace and offers practical solutions for overcoming them. It provides readers with a deeper understanding of the complex issues involved in peacebuilding and inspires them to take action in promoting peace in their own lives and communities.

This book is intended for anyone interested in promoting peace in their communities and beyond. It is a valuable resource for policymakers, scholars, activists, and anyone seeking to make a positive contribution to the world. We believe that by working together, we can overcome corruption, violence, and hatred, and create a more peaceful and just world for future generations.

C. P. Kumar
Reiki Healer
Former Scientist 'G', National Institute of Hydrology
Roorkee - 247667, India
E-mail: cpkumar@yahoo.com
Web: https://www.angelfire.com/nh/cpkumar/virgo.html

Introduction

In a world marked by conflict, unrest, and political instability, the importance of peace cannot be overstated. Peace is often defined as a state of calm or tranquility, but it encompasses much more than that. It is a state of harmony and stability that is essential for the well-being of individuals, societies, and nations. In this article, we will define peace and explore its relevance in our world today.

Defining Peace

Peace is often defined as the absence of war or conflict. However, this definition is too narrow to capture the full meaning of peace. Peace is not just the absence of violence but also the presence of social, economic, and political stability. It is a state in which individuals can live without fear, oppression, or discrimination. Peace is not just a state of mind; it is a condition that must be established and maintained through deliberate action.

Types of Peace

There are different types of peace that are relevant in our world today. The first is negative peace, which refers to the absence of violence or war. The second is positive peace, which refers to the presence of social, economic, and political stability. Positive peace is often more difficult to achieve than negative peace because it requires the establishment of a just and equitable society.

Relevance of Peace in Our World Today

Peace is essential for the well-being of individuals, societies, and nations. It is the foundation upon which prosperity, development, and progress are built. In a world marked by conflict, unrest, and political instability, peace is essential for the following reasons:

1. Economic Development

Peace is essential for economic development. In a state of peace, individuals and businesses can operate freely without fear of violence or disruption. This creates a stable and conducive environment for economic activity, leading to job creation, increased trade, and investment. Economic development, in turn, leads to higher standards of living and an improvement in the quality of life.

2. Social Justice

Peace is essential for social justice. In a state of peace, individuals are free to express themselves and pursue their aspirations without fear of oppression or discrimination. This leads to the establishment of a just and equitable society, where everyone has equal opportunities and access to resources. Social justice is essential for reducing poverty, promoting equality, and fostering a sense of community.

3. Environmental Sustainability

Peace is essential for environmental sustainability. In a state of peace, individuals and governments can work together to address environmental challenges such as climate change, pollution, and deforestation. This requires cooperation and collaboration, which is only possible in a state of peace.

4. Health and Well-being

Peace is essential for health and well-being. In a state of peace, individuals have access to basic services such as healthcare, education, and clean water. This leads to improved health outcomes and a higher quality of life. In addition, peace is essential for mental health, as individuals can live without fear and anxiety.

5. Human Rights

Peace is essential for human rights. In a state of peace, individuals have the right to freedom of expression, association, and assembly. They also have the right to live without fear of violence, oppression, or discrimination. These rights are essential for the protection of human dignity and the promotion of democracy and good governance.

Challenges to Achieving Peace

Despite the importance of peace, achieving it is not always easy. There are several challenges that must be overcome, including:

1. Conflict

Conflict is the most significant barrier to peace. Conflicts can arise from a variety of sources, including political, economic, and social factors. Conflicts can be difficult to resolve, as they often involve deeply ingrained beliefs and values. Conflict resolution requires cooperation, dialogue, and compromise.

2. Poverty

Poverty is a significant barrier to peace. Poverty can create social unrest and political instability, leading to conflict and violence. Poverty reduction is essential for promoting peace, as it creates opportunities for economic growth and development.

3. Inequality

Inequality is another significant barrier to peace. Inequality can lead to social unrest and political instability, as individuals and groups feel marginalized and excluded from society. Addressing inequality requires the establishment of a just and equitable society, where everyone has equal opportunities and access to resources.

4. Lack of Trust

Lack of trust is a significant barrier to peace. Trust is essential for cooperation and collaboration, which are necessary for addressing complex problems such as conflict and poverty. Lack of trust can be caused by historical grievances, cultural differences, or political polarization. Building trust requires dialogue, compromise, and a willingness to understand and respect different perspectives.

5. Globalization

Globalization has created both opportunities and challenges for peace. Globalization has led to increased trade, investment, and economic growth, but it has also led to increased competition and inequality. Globalization has also created new forms of conflict, such as cyber warfare and terrorism. Addressing the challenges of globalization requires global cooperation and collaboration.

Conclusion

Peace is essential for the well-being of individuals, societies, and nations. It is the foundation upon which prosperity, development, and progress are built. Peace is not just the absence of violence but also the presence of social, economic, and political stability. Achieving peace requires addressing the challenges of conflict, poverty, inequality, lack of trust, and globalization. The importance of peace cannot be overstated, and it is essential that we work together to establish and maintain it in our world today.

Introduction

Corruption has been a pervasive problem throughout history and across the world. It can manifest in various forms, such as bribery, nepotism, embezzlement, and abuse of power. Corruption affects individuals, institutions, and entire societies, undermining the rule of law, democracy, and economic development. Understanding the roots of corruption, its causes, and its effects is crucial for devising effective strategies to prevent and combat it.

What is Corruption?

Corruption can be defined as the misuse of public power for private gain. It involves the abuse of entrusted power for personal or group benefit, often at the expense of the common good. Corruption can occur in various forms, such as bribery, fraud, embezzlement, nepotism, cronyism, and abuse of power. It can affect all sectors of society, including politics, business, education, healthcare, and law enforcement.

Causes of Corruption

Corruption is a complex phenomenon influenced by various factors. Some of the common causes of corruption include:

1. Weak Institutional Frameworks: Corruption is more prevalent in countries with weak institutional frameworks, where the rule of law, checks and balances, and

accountability mechanisms are weak or non-existent. In such environments, corruption becomes a norm and a way of life.

2. Poverty and Inequality: Poverty and inequality can fuel corruption by creating opportunities for rent-seeking and patronage. When people lack access to basic services and opportunities, they may resort to corrupt practices to survive or improve their living standards.

3. Greed and Self-Interest: Corruption is often motivated by greed and self-interest, as individuals seek to maximize their personal gain at the expense of the public good. In some cases, corruption may be driven by a desire for power or status.

4. Lack of Transparency and Openness: Corruption thrives in environments with limited transparency and openness, where information is controlled and access to decision-making processes is restricted. Lack of transparency allows corrupt officials to act with impunity and evade accountability.

5. Cultural Factors: Cultural factors can also play a role in promoting or tolerating corruption. In some societies, gift-giving and personal connections are considered normal and acceptable, even if they involve corrupt practices. Such cultural norms can make it difficult to combat corruption effectively.

Effects of Corruption

The effects of corruption can be far-reaching and devastating for individuals, institutions, and societies. Some of the common effects of corruption include:

1. Undermining the Rule of Law: Corruption erodes the rule of law and undermines the legitimacy of legal and democratic institutions. When the law is not applied equally and impartially, citizens lose faith in the justice system, leading to social unrest and instability.

2. Economic Consequences: Corruption can have severe economic consequences, reducing economic growth, increasing poverty and inequality, and distorting market mechanisms. It can also discourage foreign investment and erode the credibility of the government and financial institutions.

3. Social and Political Consequences: Corruption can have profound social and political consequences, eroding trust in public institutions, and deepening social divisions. It can lead to a breakdown of social norms and values, fueling resentment and conflict.

4. Human Rights Violations: Corruption can lead to human rights violations, particularly in contexts where corrupt officials are involved in the abuse of power or repression of political dissent. Corruption can also undermine efforts to promote democracy and good governance, leading to a cycle of poverty, inequality, and oppression.

Preventing and Combating Corruption

Preventing and combating corruption requires a multi-faceted approach, involving institutional, legal, and societal measures. Some of the key strategies for preventing and combating corruption include:

1. Strengthening Institutional Frameworks: One of the most effective ways to prevent and combat corruption is to strengthen institutional frameworks, such as the rule of law,

separation of powers, and independent judiciary. This involves creating and enforcing laws that punish corrupt behavior, establishing strong regulatory bodies, and promoting transparency and accountability in government and public institutions.

2.   Promoting Economic Development: Economic development can be a powerful tool in reducing corruption. By promoting economic growth, creating job opportunities, and reducing poverty and inequality, countries can reduce the incentives for corrupt practices. This requires investing in education, infrastructure, and other critical sectors that drive economic growth.

3. Encouraging Public Participation: Public participation and civil society engagement can be instrumental in preventing and combating corruption. By promoting transparency, accountability, and citizen engagement, societies can hold public officials accountable and reduce opportunities for corrupt practices.

4. Strengthening International Cooperation: Corruption is a global problem that requires international cooperation and collaboration. By promoting cross-border cooperation, sharing best practices, and developing international legal frameworks, countries can work together to prevent and combat corruption.

5. Changing Cultural Norms: Cultural norms and values can play a significant role in promoting or tolerating corruption. By promoting values such as honesty, integrity, and transparency, societies can change cultural norms and reduce the acceptance of corrupt practices.

Conclusion

Corruption is a complex and pervasive problem that affects individuals, institutions, and entire societies. Understanding the roots of corruption, its causes, and its effects is critical for devising effective strategies to prevent and combat it. Preventing and combating corruption requires a multi-faceted approach, involving institutional, legal, and societal measures. By strengthening institutional frameworks, promoting economic development, encouraging public participation, strengthening international cooperation, and changing cultural norms, societies can reduce corruption and promote good governance, democracy, and human rights.

Introduction

Corruption in politics is a widespread problem in countries across the world. It is a phenomenon that has been around for centuries and continues to be a major issue today. Corrupt politicians use their power and influence to gain personal benefits, often at the expense of the common people. This article will examine the impact of corrupt politicians and their influence on society.

What is Corruption in Politics?

Corruption in politics is the misuse of power or public resources by politicians for personal gain. It involves bribery, fraud, embezzlement, and other illegal activities that are done to enrich oneself. Corruption in politics is a significant problem because it undermines the democratic process and results in a lack of trust in government institutions.

The Impact of Corruption on Society

1. Economic Impact: Corruption has a negative impact on the economy. When politicians engage in corrupt activities, it often results in misallocation of resources, which affects economic growth. Corruption also creates an uneven playing field, where those with power and money have an unfair advantage over others.

2. Social Impact: Corruption in politics has a significant impact on society. It creates a culture of distrust, where

people lose faith in government institutions. It also creates an environment where unethical behavior is normalized, leading to a breakdown in social values and morality.

3. Political Impact: Corruption undermines the democratic process and creates a lack of confidence in government institutions. It allows politicians to gain power and influence through unethical means, leading to a concentration of power in the hands of a few. This, in turn, makes it difficult for others to participate in the political process, leading to a lack of representation for marginalized groups.

4. Environmental Impact: Corruption in politics can also have an impact on the environment. When politicians engage in corrupt activities, they may be more likely to engage in activities that harm the environment. For example, they may allow companies to engage in activities that harm the environment in exchange for personal gain.

Measures to Tackle Corruption

1. Transparency: Transparency is a key measure to tackle corruption in politics. Governments should ensure that information about public spending is available to the public. This can be done through the use of open data, which allows citizens to access information about government spending.

2. Independent Anti-Corruption Agencies: Independent anti-corruption agencies can play an important role in tackling corruption. These agencies should have the power to investigate and prosecute corrupt politicians and officials.

3. Education: Education is an important measure to tackle corruption. Citizens should be educated about the negative impact of corruption on society and how to identify and report corrupt activities.

4. Political Reform: Political reform can help tackle corruption by creating a more transparent and accountable political system. This can include measures such as campaign finance reform, electoral reform, and the establishment of an independent judiciary.

5. Whistleblower Protection: Whistleblower protection can encourage individuals to report corruption without fear of retaliation. Governments should ensure that whistleblowers are protected and that their identities are kept confidential.

6. International Cooperation: International cooperation is important in tackling corruption. Countries should work together to prevent the flow of illicit funds across borders and to share best practices in combating corruption.

Conclusion

Corruption in politics is a serious problem that affects societies across the world. It has a negative impact on the economy, social values, and the democratic process. Corrupt politicians use their power and influence to gain personal benefits, often at the expense of the common people. It is essential to take measures to tackle corruption, such as transparency, independent anti-corruption agencies, education, political reform, whistleblower protection, and international cooperation. By working together, we can create a more transparent and accountable political system and ensure that politicians are held accountable for their actions.

Introduction

Corruption is one of the biggest obstacles to development in many countries around the world. It undermines trust in governments, erodes the rule of law, and distorts public policies to benefit a few at the expense of the many. The fight against corruption requires a multifaceted approach, including effective laws and enforcement, a free press, and an independent judiciary. However, education also plays a critical role in overcoming corruption, both as a preventive measure and as a means of empowering citizens to demand transparency and accountability from their governments.

In this article, we will explore the role of education in overcoming corruption, highlighting the importance of education in fighting corruption.

Prevention of Corruption through Education

Education can play a crucial role in preventing corruption from taking root in societies. By providing citizens with knowledge about the negative effects of corruption on society and the economy, education can help build a culture of transparency, accountability, and integrity. Education can also promote a sense of civic responsibility and encourage citizens to actively engage in anti-corruption efforts.

One way education can prevent corruption is by promoting ethical behavior among public officials. By providing education on ethical values and codes of conduct, public officials can be held accountable for their actions and held to a higher standard of behavior. This can help reduce opportunities for corruption by creating a culture of ethical behavior that is expected and enforced.

In addition, education can also help citizens identify and report corrupt behavior. By providing citizens with the knowledge and tools to recognize and report corruption, education can help create a culture of transparency and accountability. Citizens who are empowered to identify and report corruption can help deter corrupt behavior and promote integrity in government.

Empowering Citizens through Education

Education can also empower citizens to demand transparency and accountability from their governments. By providing citizens with information about their rights and responsibilities, education can help them understand how to hold their governments accountable for their actions.

Education can also promote active citizenship and participation in democratic processes. Citizens who are educated about their rights and responsibilities are more likely to engage in civil society organizations, participate in elections, and hold their governments accountable. By empowering citizens to participate in democratic processes, education can help reduce the opportunities for corruption by promoting transparency and accountability.

In addition, education can also help promote good governance by building the capacity of public officials. By providing public officials with education and training, they can acquire the knowledge and skills needed to perform their duties effectively and efficiently. This can help reduce opportunities for corruption by ensuring that public officials have the expertise needed to make informed decisions and implement policies that promote transparency and accountability.

Education as a Tool for Sustainable Development

Education is also critical for sustainable development, and the fight against corruption is no exception. Education can help promote economic growth by creating a skilled workforce and promoting innovation and entrepreneurship. This can help reduce poverty and promote prosperity, reducing the opportunities for corruption by addressing the underlying causes of inequality and economic instability.

In addition, education can help promote social inclusion and reduce discrimination. By promoting diversity and inclusion, education can help reduce the opportunities for corruption by creating a more equitable society that values and respects the rights of all individuals.

Conclusion

The fight against corruption is a complex and multifaceted challenge that requires a coordinated and sustained effort from all sectors of society. Education can play a critical role in overcoming corruption, both as a preventive measure and as a means of empowering citizens to demand transparency and accountability from their governments. By promoting ethical behavior among public officials, empowering citizens to participate in democratic processes, and promoting sustainable development, education can help reduce the opportunities for corruption and build a more transparent, accountable, and inclusive society. As such, investing in education is an investment in the future of our societies and the well-being of our citizens.

Introduction

Violence is a social phenomenon that affects individuals, groups, and entire societies. It is a multifaceted and complex issue that has various forms and affects people differently. Understanding the different types of violence and their impact on society is essential to addressing this problem. In this article, we will examine the various forms of violence and their impact on society.

Types of Violence

1. Physical Violence: Physical violence is the most visible and recognizable form of violence. It is any form of violence that causes bodily harm, such as hitting, kicking, punching, or using weapons. Physical violence can be used as a means of control or domination over someone, or it can be a result of personal frustration or anger. The impact of physical violence can be severe, resulting in long-term physical and psychological harm.

2. Sexual Violence: Sexual violence is any form of non-consensual sexual activity. It can include rape, sexual assault, sexual harassment, and any other form of unwanted sexual contact. Sexual violence is often used as a means of control and domination over someone, particularly women and children. The impact of sexual violence can be severe, resulting in long-term physical and psychological harm.

3. Emotional Violence: Emotional violence is any form of abuse that causes emotional harm. It can include verbal

abuse, psychological abuse, and emotional manipulation. Emotional violence can be a result of controlling behavior or a way to exert power over someone. The impact of emotional violence can be severe, resulting in long-term emotional and psychological harm.

4. Economic Violence: Economic violence is any form of abuse that causes financial harm. It can include withholding money, limiting access to resources, and using economic power to control or manipulate someone. Economic violence can be a form of domestic abuse or can occur in the workplace or other settings. The impact of economic violence can be severe, resulting in long-term financial and psychological harm.

5. Structural Violence: Structural violence is a form of violence that is embedded in social structures and institutions. It can include discrimination based on race, gender, or socioeconomic status, as well as systemic inequality and oppression. Structural violence can be a result of political and economic policies that disadvantage certain groups. The impact of structural violence can be severe, resulting in long-term social, economic, and political harm.

Impact of Violence on Society

1. Physical and Psychological Harm: Violence can cause physical harm, such as injuries, disabilities, and even death. It can also cause psychological harm, such as trauma, anxiety, depression, and post-traumatic stress disorder (PTSD). The impact of violence can be long-lasting and can affect the well-being of individuals and society as a whole.

2. Economic Cost: Violence can have a significant economic cost, both direct and indirect. The direct cost includes medical expenses, legal fees, and other expenses associated with addressing the immediate consequences of violence. The indirect cost includes lost productivity, decreased quality of life, and other long-term economic consequences.

3. Social and Cultural Impact: Violence can also have a significant social and cultural impact. It can create fear, mistrust, and a sense of insecurity in society. It can also perpetuate stereotypes and perpetuate social inequality and oppression. The impact of violence can be felt across generations and can affect the overall social fabric of a society.

Prevention and Intervention

Preventing and addressing violence requires a multi-faceted approach that includes education, awareness-raising, policy changes, and community engagement. Some strategies for preventing and addressing violence include:

1. Education and Awareness-raising: Educating people about the different types of violence and their impact on society can help prevent violence. It can also help raise awareness about the resources and support available to those affected by violence.

2. Policy Changes: Changes in policies and laws can help prevent violence by addressing the root causes of violence. For example, policies and laws can be put in place to address economic inequality and discrimination. Laws can also be put in place to protect victims of violence and hold perpetrators accountable for their actions.

3. Community Engagement: **Engaging with communities can help prevent violence by promoting social cohesion and addressing the underlying social and economic factors that contribute to violence. This can include programs that promote community involvement, such as neighborhood watch programs, and initiatives that provide resources and support to vulnerable populations.**

4. Rehabilitation and Support: **Providing support and rehabilitation to victims of violence can help them recover and prevent them from becoming perpetrators of violence themselves. This can include counseling and therapy, as well as programs that provide economic and social support.**

Conclusion

Violence is a complex issue that affects individuals, groups, and entire societies. Understanding the different types of violence and their impact on society is essential to addressing this problem. Violence can cause physical, psychological, economic, social, and cultural harm, and preventing and addressing violence requires a multi-faceted approach that includes education, awareness-raising, policy changes, and community engagement. By working together, we can create a safer and more peaceful society for all.

Introduction

Violence is a global phenomenon that has been a major concern throughout human history. It manifests in different forms such as physical, emotional, psychological, economic, and sexual violence. Violence has devastating consequences on individuals, communities, and societies. It leads to injuries, disabilities, deaths, psychological trauma, and social disruption. Violence also hinders economic development, creates inequality, and undermines human rights.

Identifying the underlying causes of violence is essential for addressing the problem. This article explores the roots of violence and how to address them.

Poverty and Inequality

Poverty and inequality are among the major causes of violence. Poverty creates a fertile ground for violence to thrive. Poor people are more vulnerable to violence as they lack access to basic needs such as food, shelter, healthcare, and education. Poverty also creates desperation, frustration, and hopelessness, which can lead to violent behavior. People who live in poverty often lack opportunities to improve their lives and may turn to criminal activities or violent behavior as a means of survival.

Inequality, on the other hand, creates a sense of injustice, resentment, and anger among those who are excluded from the benefits of society. This can lead to violent protests, riots, and revolutions. Inequality also creates a culture of violence where people are more likely to use violence to resolve conflicts or disputes. Addressing poverty and inequality requires social and economic policies that promote equality, justice, and inclusion.

Cultural and Social Norms

Cultural and social norms also play a significant role in promoting or preventing violence. In some cultures, violence is accepted or even glorified as a means of resolving conflicts or asserting power. This can lead to domestic violence, sexual violence, and community violence. Social norms that promote aggression, dominance, and control can also contribute to violence.

Changing cultural and social norms requires a long-term and comprehensive approach that involves education, awareness-raising, and community mobilization. It also requires engaging with cultural and religious leaders to promote peaceful and non-violent values.

Mental Health and Substance Abuse

Mental health and substance abuse are also significant underlying causes of violence. People with mental health problems such as depression, anxiety, and schizophrenia are more likely to engage in violent behavior. Substance abuse, including alcohol and drugs, can also lead to violent behavior.

Addressing mental health and substance abuse requires adequate resources and services for prevention, treatment, and support. It also requires reducing stigma and discrimination associated with mental health and substance abuse.

Political and Economic Instability

Political and economic instability can also contribute to violence. In countries where there is a lack of political stability, conflict, or civil war, violence becomes widespread. Economic instability, including unemployment and poverty, can also lead to violent behavior.

Addressing political and economic instability requires promoting peace, stability, and democracy. It also requires creating opportunities for economic growth and development.

Lack of Access to Justice

Lack of access to justice can also contribute to violence. When people feel that they cannot access justice through the legal system, they may resort to violence to seek revenge or justice. This can lead to vigilantism, lynching, and mob justice.

Addressing lack of access to justice requires ensuring that the legal system is accessible, affordable, and fair. It also requires promoting alternative dispute resolution mechanisms such as mediation and arbitration.

Gender Inequality

Gender inequality is a significant underlying cause of violence against women and girls. Gender-based violence, including domestic violence, sexual violence, and harassment, is prevalent in all societies. Gender inequality creates power imbalances between men and women that can lead to violence.

Addressing gender inequality requires promoting gender equality and women's empowerment. It also requires challenging harmful gender norms and stereotypes that perpetuate gender-based violence.

How to Address the Root Causes of Violence

Addressing the root causes of violence requires a multi-faceted approach that involves different sectors and stakeholders. Here are some strategies that can be employed:

1. Strengthening social and economic policies: Social and economic policies that promote equality, justice, and inclusion are essential for addressing poverty and inequality. These policies can include social protection programs, fair labor practices, and progressive taxation.

2. Promoting education and awareness: Education and awareness-raising campaigns can help change cultural and social norms that perpetuate violence. This can include programs that promote peaceful and non-violent values, as well as campaigns that challenge harmful gender norms and stereotypes.

3. Investing in mental health and substance abuse services: Adequate resources and services for prevention, treatment, and support for mental health and substance abuse are essential for addressing these underlying causes of violence.

4. Promoting peace, stability, and democracy: Political and economic instability can contribute to violence, making promoting peace, stability, and democracy important for preventing violence.

5. Ensuring access to justice: Ensuring that the legal system is accessible, affordable, and fair can help prevent vigilantism, lynching, and mob justice.

6. Empowering women and promoting gender equality: Empowering women and promoting gender equality can help prevent gender-based violence and create a more equal and just society.

Conclusion

Violence is a complex and multi-faceted problem that requires a comprehensive approach to address its root causes. Poverty and inequality, cultural and social norms, mental health and substance abuse, political and economic instability, lack of access to justice, and gender inequality are some of the underlying causes of violence that need to be addressed. Strategies such as strengthening social and economic policies, promoting education and awareness, investing in mental health and substance abuse services, promoting peace, stability, and democracy, ensuring access to justice, and empowering women and promoting gender equality can help prevent violence and create a more peaceful and just society.

Introduction

Violence is a destructive force that has caused significant damage to humanity throughout history. It is not just physical harm, but also psychological and emotional damage. Violence can occur in many forms, such as domestic violence, gang violence, terrorism, and warfare, and can be inflicted on individuals, communities, or even whole countries. Preventing violence and promoting peace are crucial for creating a safer and more peaceful society. In this article, we will explore different methods for preventing violence and promoting peace.

1. Education and Awareness

Education and awareness are essential for preventing violence. People who are educated and aware of the consequences of violence are less likely to engage in violent behavior. Education can help individuals develop critical thinking skills and empathy, which are necessary for understanding the impact of violence on others. It can also help them recognize the signs of violence and how to prevent it.

Awareness campaigns can be useful in educating the public about the effects of violence and promoting peace. These campaigns can be targeted towards specific groups, such as schools, youth, or communities affected by violence. They can include public service announcements, social media campaigns, and community events. For example, campaigns can be focused on ending gender-based violence or reducing gun violence.

2. Conflict Resolution

Conflict resolution is a process that helps individuals or groups to peacefully resolve conflicts. It involves identifying the root cause of the conflict, listening to all parties involved, and finding a solution that meets everyone's needs. Conflict resolution can help prevent violence by addressing conflicts before they escalate into violent behavior.

There are many approaches to conflict resolution, such as negotiation, mediation, and restorative justice. Negotiation involves two parties coming together to find a mutually acceptable solution. Mediation involves a third party who helps facilitate communication between the parties and find a solution that meets everyone's needs. Restorative justice is a process that involves the offender, the victim, and the community in finding a solution that repairs the harm caused by the offense.

3. Strengthening Communities

Strengthening communities is a crucial step in preventing violence. Communities that are strong and connected are less likely to experience violence. Strong communities provide social support, positive role models, and opportunities for people to engage in positive activities.

One way to strengthen communities is by promoting community engagement. This can be achieved through community events, volunteer opportunities, and community-based organizations. Community engagement helps people develop a sense of belonging and connection, which can help prevent violence.

Another way to strengthen communities is by promoting economic development. Poverty and economic inequality are significant factors that contribute to violence. By promoting economic development, communities can provide more opportunities for people to succeed and reduce the likelihood of violence.

4. Addressing Mental Health

Mental health is a significant factor that contributes to violence. People who are suffering from mental health issues are more likely to engage in violent behavior. Addressing mental health issues is crucial for preventing violence.

One way to address mental health is by providing access to mental health services. Mental health services can include counseling, therapy, and medication. Access to mental health services can help individuals manage their mental health issues and reduce the likelihood of violent behavior.

Another way to address mental health is by reducing the stigma associated with mental illness. Stigma can prevent people from seeking help and can contribute to feelings of isolation and hopelessness. By reducing the stigma associated with mental illness, more people may be willing to seek help and receive the support they need.

5. Gun Control

Gun violence is a significant problem in many parts of the world. Gun control measures can help prevent gun violence and promote peace. Gun control measures can include background checks, waiting periods, and restrictions on the types of guns that can be owned.

Background checks can help prevent people who are not legally allowed to own guns from obtaining them. Waiting periods can help prevent impulsive acts of violence by giving individuals time to cool down and think before obtaining a gun. Restrictions on the types of guns that can be owned can help reduce the number of guns available and the likelihood of gun violence.

6. International Cooperation

Violence is not limited to one country or region. International cooperation is necessary for preventing violence and promoting peace globally. Countries can work together to address issues such as terrorism, war, and human rights violations.

International cooperation can take many forms, such as diplomatic negotiations, economic sanctions, and military interventions. Diplomatic negotiations involve countries working together to find peaceful solutions to conflicts. Economic sanctions can be used to pressure countries to change their behavior. Military interventions can be used as a last resort to prevent human rights violations or genocide.

7. Empowering Women and Girls

Empowering women and girls is essential for preventing violence. Women and girls are often the most vulnerable to violence, including domestic violence and gender-based violence. Empowering women and girls can help reduce their vulnerability to violence and promote gender equality.

Empowering women and girls can be achieved through education, employment opportunities, and access to healthcare. Education can help girls develop critical thinking skills and gain knowledge about their rights. Employment opportunities can provide financial independence and reduce their reliance on abusive partners. Access to healthcare can help address health issues that contribute to vulnerability, such as reproductive health.

Conclusion

Preventing violence and promoting peace are crucial for creating a safer and more peaceful society. Education and awareness, conflict resolution, strengthening communities, addressing mental health, gun control, international cooperation, and empowering women and girls are all methods that can be used to prevent violence and promote peace. It is essential to address the root causes of violence and work towards creating a society that values peace and non-violence. By working together, we can create a safer and more peaceful world for everyone.

Introduction

Forgiveness is a powerful tool that can help individuals and societies overcome hatred and promote peace. It involves letting go of feelings of anger, resentment, and the desire for revenge against someone who has wronged us. Forgiveness can be difficult, but it is essential for healing and moving forward in life. In this article, we will explore the power of forgiveness, its role in overcoming hatred, and its ability to promote peace.

The Nature of Forgiveness

Forgiveness is a complex and multifaceted concept. At its core, forgiveness involves letting go of negative emotions toward someone who has hurt us. It is a decision to no longer hold onto anger, resentment, or the desire for revenge. Forgiveness does not mean forgetting the harm that was done or excusing the offender's behavior. Instead, it is a way to release ourselves from the burden of holding onto negative emotions and to move forward in a more positive direction.

Forgiveness is not always easy, and it can take time to achieve. In some cases, forgiveness may involve a process of working through feelings of anger and hurt, seeking support from others, and learning to see the situation from different perspectives. In other cases, forgiveness may come more easily, especially if the harm done was unintentional or if the offender has taken steps to make amends.

The Power of Forgiveness

The power of forgiveness lies in its ability to heal emotional wounds and promote positive outcomes. Forgiveness has been linked to lower levels of stress, anxiety, and depression, as well as higher levels of happiness and life satisfaction. Studies have also found that forgiveness can improve relationships, increase empathy and compassion, and promote prosocial behavior.

One reason forgiveness is so powerful is that it allows individuals to break free from the cycle of negative emotions and behaviors that can perpetuate harm and conflict. When we hold onto feelings of anger and resentment, we may become more defensive, less open to alternative perspectives, and more likely to engage in retaliatory actions. By contrast, when we forgive, we open ourselves up to the possibility of reconciliation, understanding, and healing.

Forgiveness and Overcoming Hatred

One of the most profound ways that forgiveness can promote peace is by helping individuals overcome hatred. Hatred is a powerful and destructive emotion that can lead to prejudice, discrimination, and even violence. When we hate someone, we view them as fundamentally different from ourselves, and we may dehumanize or demonize them. This can make it easier to justify acts of aggression or harm.

Forgiveness can challenge this cycle of hatred by promoting empathy, understanding, and connection. When we forgive someone, we are acknowledging their humanity and recognizing that they are capable of both good and bad behavior. We are also acknowledging our own fallibility and recognizing that we too are capable of causing harm. In this way, forgiveness can promote a sense of shared humanity and interconnectedness that can help break down barriers and reduce prejudice.

Forgiveness can also help individuals and societies overcome the legacy of past injustices. When we hold onto feelings of anger and resentment over past wrongs, we may perpetuate cycles of violence and conflict. By contrast, when we forgive, we can open up the possibility of reconciliation, healing, and renewed relationships. Forgiveness can help break down barriers between groups and promote a sense of shared humanity and common purpose.

Forgiveness and Promoting Peace

Forgiveness can also play a crucial role in promoting peace on a societal level. In conflict-affected societies, forgiveness can be a powerful tool for healing and reconciliation. By acknowledging past wrongs, seeking forgiveness, and offering forgiveness to others, individuals and societies can break down barriers and promote mutual understanding and cooperation.

One example of this is the Truth and Reconciliation Commission in South Africa. The commission was established in 1995 to help heal the wounds of apartheid and promote reconciliation between different racial groups. The commission provided a platform for victims and perpetrators of violence to share their stories, seek forgiveness, and offer forgiveness to others. This process helped break down barriers and promote healing and understanding, even in the face of deep-seated divisions.

Forgiveness can also play a role in preventing conflict in the first place. When individuals and societies are able to forgive past wrongs and let go of feelings of anger and resentment, they may be less likely to engage in retaliatory actions. Forgiveness can also promote empathy and compassion, making it easier for individuals to see the perspectives of others and work towards mutually beneficial outcomes.

Challenges to Forgiveness

While forgiveness can be a powerful tool for promoting peace and overcoming hatred, it is not always easy to achieve. There are many challenges to forgiveness, including feelings of anger and resentment, a desire for revenge, and a fear of vulnerability. Additionally, forgiveness may be more difficult in situations where harm was intentional or severe, or when the offender has not taken steps to make amends.

Despite these challenges, forgiveness is often essential for healing and moving forward. In some cases, forgiveness may involve a process of working through negative emotions and seeking support from others. It may also involve setting boundaries and taking steps to protect oneself from further harm. In other cases, forgiveness may come more easily, especially if the offender has shown remorse or taken steps to make amends.

Conclusion

Forgiveness is a powerful tool that can help individuals and societies overcome hatred and promote peace. By letting go of negative emotions and seeking understanding and connection with others, forgiveness can promote healing, reconciliation, and renewed relationships. While forgiveness may be difficult to achieve, it is often essential for moving forward and achieving a more positive and peaceful future. As we work towards building a more just and peaceful world, forgiveness must be an essential part of our toolkit.

Introduction

Hatred is a strong and intense feeling of dislike or animosity towards someone or something. It is a common emotion that many people experience throughout their lives. However, when hatred is taken to an extreme level, it can have devastating consequences, leading to acts of violence, discrimination, and prejudice. To overcome hatred, it is important to examine the root causes of this emotion and identify effective ways to address it.

What are the root causes of hatred?

Hatred can have many root causes, including personal experiences, cultural and societal norms, and psychological factors. Personal experiences such as being bullied, discriminated against, or victimized can lead to feelings of hatred towards individuals or groups. Cultural and societal norms that promote prejudice and discrimination can also contribute to the development of hatred towards certain groups, such as those based on race, religion, gender, or sexual orientation. Psychological factors, such as fear, insecurity, and a need for power, can also fuel feelings of hatred towards others.

How does hatred manifest?

Hatred can manifest in many ways, ranging from subtle forms of prejudice to extreme acts of violence. Some examples of subtle forms of prejudice include microaggressions, such as making assumptions about someone based on their race or ethnicity, or excluding someone from a social group because of their religion or sexual orientation. More extreme forms of hatred include hate crimes, such as physical assaults or verbal abuse, and acts of terrorism or genocide.

How can we overcome hatred?

Overcoming hatred is a complex process that requires a multifaceted approach. Here are some strategies that can help:

1. Develop empathy

Empathy is the ability to understand and share the feelings of another person. Developing empathy towards others can help to reduce feelings of hatred and increase understanding and tolerance. One way to develop empathy is to actively listen to others and try to see things from their perspective. This can help to break down stereotypes and assumptions and create a more open and inclusive environment.

2. Address personal biases

Personal biases and prejudices can contribute to feelings of hatred towards others. It is important to be aware of our own biases and work to address them. This can be done through self-reflection, education, and exposure to diverse perspectives and experiences.

3. Speak out against hate

Silence can contribute to the normalization of hatred and prejudice. Speaking out against hate and prejudice can help to create a more inclusive and tolerant society. This can be done through social media, community events, or by taking action to support marginalized groups.

4. Educate yourself and others

Education is a powerful tool in overcoming hatred. By learning about the experiences and perspectives of others, we can develop a greater understanding and empathy towards them. Educating others can also help to break down stereotypes and promote tolerance.

5. Practice forgiveness

Forgiveness can be a difficult but powerful tool in overcoming hatred. Forgiving those who have wronged us can help to release feelings of anger and bitterness and promote healing. It is important to note that forgiveness does not mean forgetting or excusing harmful behavior, but rather choosing to let go of negative emotions and move forward.

6. Seek professional help

For those who have experienced significant trauma or are struggling with intense feelings of hatred, seeking professional help can be a beneficial step towards healing. Therapists and counselors can provide support and guidance in managing emotions and developing coping strategies.

Conclusion

Overcoming hatred is a complex and multifaceted process that requires a combination of personal and societal changes. By developing empathy, addressing personal biases, speaking out against hate, educating ourselves and others, practicing forgiveness, and seeking professional help when needed, we can work towards creating a more inclusive and tolerant society. It is important to remember that change takes time and effort, but with persistence and dedication, we can overcome hatred and create a better world for all.

Introduction

Empathy is the ability to understand and share the feelings of others. It is an essential trait that allows us to connect with people and establish meaningful relationships. Empathy helps us to understand people's perspectives, and this understanding can lead to a better world. In this article, we will highlight the importance of empathy in promoting understanding and peace.

Empathy builds trust and respect

Empathy builds trust and respect, two essential components for peaceful relationships. When we are empathetic, we show that we care about others and their well-being. We take the time to understand their point of view and try to see things from their perspective. This helps to create a sense of trust, which is vital in any relationship. When people feel that they are understood and valued, they are more likely to open up and share their thoughts and feelings. This, in turn, can lead to a deeper connection and a stronger bond between people.

Empathy promotes understanding

Empathy promotes understanding, and understanding is the key to peaceful coexistence. When we take the time to understand others, we can bridge the gap between us and them. We can find common ground and work together towards a shared goal. Empathy allows us to see things from different perspectives, which can be helpful in finding solutions to complex problems. When we can see things from multiple angles, we are more likely to come up with creative solutions that benefit everyone.

Empathy reduces conflict

Empathy reduces conflict because it allows us to see things from the other person's point of view. When we can understand why someone is upset or angry, we are less likely to react defensively. Instead, we can respond in a way that is more constructive and helpful. Empathy helps us to communicate better, and good communication is essential for resolving conflicts. When we can communicate effectively, we can find solutions that are acceptable to all parties involved.

Empathy promotes kindness and compassion

Empathy promotes kindness and compassion, two traits that are essential for promoting peace. When we are kind and compassionate, we create a positive environment that is conducive to peaceful relationships. We show that we care about others and are willing to help them when they are in need. Kindness and compassion can be contagious, and when we show these traits, others are more likely to do the same.

Empathy promotes diversity and inclusivity

Empathy promotes diversity and inclusivity by allowing us to appreciate and value differences. When we can understand and accept differences, we are more likely to create an environment that is inclusive and welcoming to all. Empathy helps us to appreciate different cultures, beliefs, and values. This, in turn, can lead to a more tolerant and accepting society where people can live together peacefully.

Empathy promotes personal growth and self-awareness

Empathy promotes personal growth and self-awareness by allowing us to see things from a different perspective. When we can understand others, we can also learn more about ourselves. Empathy helps us to see our strengths and weaknesses and to understand how our actions affect others. This self-awareness can lead to personal growth and development. When we are more self-aware, we are more likely to make better choices and to behave in a way that is more aligned with our values.

Conclusion

Empathy is an essential trait that promotes understanding and peace. Empathy allows us to connect with others, to see things from their perspective, and to appreciate their differences. Empathy promotes trust, respect, kindness, and compassion, all of which are essential for peaceful relationships. When we are empathetic, we can reduce conflict, promote diversity and inclusivity, and encourage personal growth and self-awareness. It is essential that we cultivate empathy in ourselves and in others, as it is the key to a better world.

Introduction

Religion has been a part of human society for thousands of years, and its influence on social, cultural, and political life cannot be overlooked. Throughout history, religion has played a crucial role in shaping human behavior and shaping societies. Religion has also been associated with conflict, violence, and wars. However, religion has also been a powerful force for peace and reconciliation, especially in times of conflict and war. This article explores the role of religion in peacebuilding and examines how religion can promote peace and overcome conflicts.

The Roots of Religious Conflict

Religious conflict is not a new phenomenon. Throughout history, religions have been associated with conflicts, violence, and wars. The roots of religious conflicts can be traced back to the early history of human civilization, when different religious groups developed their beliefs and practices. These differences often led to conflicts and tensions between different religious groups, leading to violence and wars. Today, religious conflicts continue to be a major challenge in many parts of the world. Religious conflicts can arise due to differences in religious beliefs, practices, and values, as well as socio-economic, political, and cultural factors.

Religion and Peacebuilding

Despite its association with conflicts and violence, religion has also been a powerful force for peace and reconciliation. Religious leaders and institutions have played a crucial role in promoting peace and overcoming conflicts in many parts of the world. Religion can promote peace by providing a sense of belonging and identity to individuals and communities. Religion can also promote values such as forgiveness, compassion, and love, which are essential for building peaceful and harmonious societies.

Religious leaders and institutions can play a crucial role in peacebuilding by promoting interfaith dialogue and cooperation. Interfaith dialogue is a process of communication and understanding between different religious groups. Through interfaith dialogue, religious leaders can promote understanding and respect for different religious beliefs and practices. Interfaith dialogue can also help to reduce tensions and conflicts between different religious groups.

Religious institutions can also play a crucial role in promoting peace and reconciliation by providing spiritual and emotional support to individuals and communities affected by conflicts. Religious institutions can provide counseling and support services to victims of violence and trauma. They can also provide education and training on conflict resolution and peacebuilding.

Case Study: The Role of Religion in Peacebuilding in Northern Ireland

The conflict in Northern Ireland, known as "The Troubles," lasted for more than three decades and claimed the lives of more than 3,500 people. The conflict was rooted in political, social, and economic factors, as well as religious differences between Protestants and Catholics.

Religion played a crucial role in the conflict, as it provided a source of identity and belonging for both communities. However, religion also exacerbated the conflict, as religious differences were often used as a justification for violence and discrimination.

Despite the role of religion in the conflict, religion also played a crucial role in peacebuilding in Northern Ireland. Religious leaders and institutions played a crucial role in promoting peace and reconciliation between the two communities.

One example of the role of religion in peacebuilding in Northern Ireland is the work of the Corrymeela Community. The Corrymeela Community is a Christian community that promotes peace and reconciliation between Protestants and Catholics in Northern Ireland. The community was founded in 1965 and has played a crucial role in peacebuilding in Northern Ireland.

The Corrymeela Community promotes peace and reconciliation through interfaith dialogue, education, and community-building activities. The community provides a safe space for individuals and communities affected by the conflict to come together, share their stories, and build relationships based on trust and respect.

The community also provides counseling and support services to victims of violence and trauma. The community's work has helped to reduce tensions and promote understanding and respect between the two communities.

Religion and Conflict Resolution

Religion can also play a crucial role in conflict resolution. Conflict resolution is the process of addressing conflicts through peaceful and nonviolent means. Religion can provide a framework for conflict resolution by promoting values such as forgiveness, compassion, and love. Religion can also provide guidance on how to address conflicts through peaceful means, such as mediation, negotiation, and dialogue.

Religious leaders and institutions can play a crucial role in conflict resolution by promoting dialogue and cooperation between conflicting parties. Religious leaders can use their moral authority to encourage conflicting parties to come to the negotiating table and find peaceful solutions to their conflicts. Religious institutions can also provide a safe and neutral space for conflicting parties to meet and engage in dialogue.

Case Study: The Role of Religion in Conflict Resolution in Liberia

The civil war in Liberia, which lasted from 1989 to 2003, claimed the lives of more than 200,000 people and displaced more than a million people. The conflict was rooted in political, social, and economic factors, as well as ethnic and religious differences between different groups.

Religion played a crucial role in the conflict, as it provided a source of identity and belonging for different ethnic and religious groups. However, religion also played a crucial role in conflict resolution in Liberia.

One example of the role of religion in conflict resolution in Liberia is the work of the Inter-Religious Council of

Liberia (IRCL). The IRCL is an interfaith organization that brings together religious leaders from different faiths to promote peace and reconciliation in Liberia.

During the civil war, the IRCL played a crucial role in mediating between conflicting parties and promoting dialogue and cooperation between different ethnic and religious groups. The IRCL used its moral authority to encourage conflicting parties to come to the negotiating table and find peaceful solutions to their conflicts.

The IRCL also played a crucial role in providing humanitarian assistance to victims of the conflict. The organization provided food, shelter, and medical assistance to people affected by the conflict, regardless of their ethnic or religious affiliation.

Religion and Post-Conflict Reconstruction

Religion can also play a crucial role in post-conflict reconstruction. Post-conflict reconstruction is the process of rebuilding societies and communities affected by conflicts. Religion can provide a framework for post-conflict reconstruction by promoting values such as forgiveness, reconciliation, and social justice.

Religious leaders and institutions can play a crucial role in post-conflict reconstruction by promoting reconciliation and healing between conflicting parties. Religious leaders can use their moral authority to encourage conflicting parties to forgive each other and move on from the past. Religious institutions can also provide counseling and support services to victims of violence and trauma.

Religion can also play a crucial role in promoting social justice and addressing the root causes of conflicts. Religion can provide guidance on how to address social, economic, and political inequalities and promote social justice and equality.

The genocide in Rwanda, which lasted for three months in 1994, claimed the lives of more than 800,000 people. The genocide was rooted in ethnic and political differences between the Hutu and Tutsi ethnic groups.

Religion played a complex role in the genocide, as religious leaders and institutions were both complicit in the violence and played a crucial role in promoting reconciliation and healing after the genocide.

One example of the role of religion in post-conflict reconstruction in Rwanda is the work of the Assemblies of God Church. The Assemblies of God Church is a Christian church that played a crucial role in promoting reconciliation and healing between the Hutu and Tutsi ethnic groups in Rwanda.

The church provided counseling and support services to victims of the genocide, as well as to perpetrators of the violence. The church also promoted forgiveness and reconciliation between the two groups, encouraging them to move on from the past and work towards a peaceful future.

Conclusion

Religion can play a crucial role in promoting peace and overcoming conflict. It can provide a framework for conflict resolution and post-conflict reconstruction by promoting values such as forgiveness, compassion, and social justice. Religious leaders and institutions can play a crucial role in promoting dialogue and cooperation between conflicting parties, as well as in promoting reconciliation and healing after conflicts.

However, it is important to note that religion can also be a source of conflict and violence. Religious differences can be used to justify violence and discrimination against members of different religious groups. Religious institutions and leaders can also be complicit in conflicts by promoting hatred and division between different religious groups.

Therefore, it is crucial to promote interfaith dialogue and cooperation and to ensure that religious leaders and institutions promote peace, reconciliation, and social justice. It is also important to ensure that religion is not used as a tool for political gain or to justify violence and discrimination against members of different religious groups.

In conclusion, the role of religion in peacebuilding is complex and multifaceted. While religion can be a source of conflict, it can also play a crucial role in promoting peace and overcoming conflicts. By promoting interfaith dialogue and cooperation and by ensuring that religious leaders and institutions promote peace, reconciliation, and social justice, we can harness the power of religion to promote a more peaceful and just world.

Introduction

Dialogue is an essential tool for resolving conflicts and promoting peace. It enables individuals, groups, and nations to exchange ideas, listen to opposing views, and work towards common goals. The importance of dialogue in conflict resolution and peacebuilding cannot be overstated. This article will discuss the role of dialogue in resolving conflicts and promoting peace.

Defining Dialogue

Dialogue is a process of communication that involves two or more parties who exchange information, ideas, and opinions to reach a common understanding or solve a problem. It is a structured and respectful conversation that promotes mutual understanding and cooperation. Dialogue can take many forms, including formal negotiations, informal conversations, and facilitated discussions.

The Role of Dialogue in Conflict Resolution

Conflict is an inevitable part of human interaction. However, dialogue can help prevent conflict from escalating and lead to a peaceful resolution. When people engage in dialogue, they have the opportunity to listen to different perspectives and find common ground. Dialogue helps to build trust and understanding, which are essential for resolving conflicts peacefully.

In conflict resolution, dialogue is particularly important because it allows the parties involved to express their concerns, fears, and aspirations. By sharing their thoughts and feelings, individuals can gain a better understanding of each other's perspectives, which can help to identify the root causes of the conflict. Once the root causes are identified, the parties can work together to find a mutually acceptable solution.

Dialogue also helps to reduce tensions and emotions that can fuel conflicts. When people are angry or frustrated, they may resort to violence or aggression. However, when they have the opportunity to express themselves through dialogue, they are less likely to act out in harmful ways.

The Role of Dialogue in Peacebuilding

Peacebuilding is a process that involves creating the conditions for sustainable peace. Dialogue plays a critical role in peacebuilding by fostering understanding and cooperation between individuals, groups, and nations.

Through dialogue, people can learn about different cultures, beliefs, and perspectives. This knowledge can help to reduce prejudice and stereotypes, which can lead to conflict. Dialogue also helps to build relationships between people who may have had little contact with each other in the past. By establishing connections, people can work together towards common goals, such as economic development or social justice.

In peacebuilding, dialogue is also essential for promoting reconciliation. When people have been harmed by conflict, they may feel a deep sense of anger or resentment. However, through dialogue, they can express their emotions and work towards forgiveness and healing. By acknowledging the pain and suffering of others, people can begin to rebuild trust and move towards a more peaceful future.

The Importance of Respectful Dialogue

Effective dialogue requires respectful communication. When people engage in dialogue, they should listen carefully to each other and avoid interrupting or dismissing opposing views. Respectful dialogue also involves acknowledging the emotions and feelings of others. By showing empathy and compassion, people can build trust and create a safe space for open and honest communication.

Respectful dialogue also requires that people approach conversations with an open mind. It is essential to be willing to consider new perspectives and ideas, even if they challenge our existing beliefs. By being open to new ideas, we can expand our understanding of the world and work towards solutions that benefit everyone.

The Challenges of Dialogue

Dialogue is not always easy. It can be challenging to engage in respectful conversation with people who hold different beliefs or perspectives. However, it is essential to recognize the value of dialogue and to be willing to put in the effort required to overcome these challenges.

One of the most significant challenges of dialogue is the fear of vulnerability. When people engage in dialogue, they may feel exposed or vulnerable. However, it is essential to recognize that vulnerability is a necessary part of dialogue. By sharing our thoughts and feelings with others, we create an environment of trust and openness that can lead to meaningful change.

Another challenge of dialogue is the tendency to demonize or stereotype those with opposing views. When people view others as the enemy, it can be difficult to engage in constructive dialogue. However, it is important to remember that everyone has their own unique experiences and perspectives. By taking the time to understand these perspectives, we can work towards finding common ground.

Finally, dialogue can be challenging because it requires patience and perseverance. Conflict resolution and peacebuilding are complex processes that can take time to achieve. However, by remaining committed to dialogue and working towards common goals, individuals and groups can create positive change.

Conclusion

Dialogue is an essential tool for resolving conflicts and promoting peace. It allows individuals, groups, and nations to exchange ideas, listen to opposing views, and work towards common goals. Dialogue is particularly important in conflict resolution because it allows the parties involved to express their concerns and find common ground. In peacebuilding, dialogue fosters understanding and cooperation between individuals, groups, and nations. To engage in effective dialogue, it is essential to approach conversations with respect, empathy, and an open mind. While dialogue can be challenging, it is an essential part of creating a more peaceful world.

Introduction

Trust is an essential component of any healthy relationship or community. Whether it's personal relationships, business partnerships, or community bonds, trust lays the foundation for cooperation, collaboration, and success. Building trust takes time, effort, and patience, but it is crucial for the longevity and sustainability of any relationship. In this article, we will explore different methods for building trust among individuals and communities.

1. Communication

Effective communication is the cornerstone of building trust. Communication involves not just speaking, but also active listening. When people feel heard and understood, they are more likely to trust the other person. It's essential to communicate clearly, honestly, and transparently to avoid misunderstandings and miscommunications. Clear communication helps to establish expectations, boundaries, and goals, which are all crucial for building trust.

2. Consistency

Consistency is key when it comes to building trust. Consistent actions, behaviors, and words create a sense of predictability and stability. When people can predict how someone will behave or react in a given situation, they are more likely to trust them. Consistency also shows that someone is reliable and dependable, which are traits that people value in others.

3. Integrity

Integrity is the foundation of trust. Integrity means doing the right thing, even when no one is watching. It involves being honest, ethical, and transparent in all actions and decisions. People who have integrity are more likely to be trusted because they are perceived as trustworthy and reliable. Demonstrating integrity builds trust over time, as people observe someone's actions and see that they consistently act with integrity.

4. Vulnerability

Vulnerability is an essential component of building trust. When people are vulnerable, they show their authentic selves, including their flaws, weaknesses, and mistakes. When people see someone else's vulnerability, they are more likely to trust them because it creates a sense of empathy and connection. Vulnerability also shows that someone is willing to take risks, be honest, and admit when they are wrong, which are all traits that people value in others.

5. Respect

Respect is crucial for building trust. Showing respect means treating others with dignity, empathy, and kindness. It involves listening to others' opinions, beliefs, and values, even if they differ from your own. Respect also means being mindful of other people's feelings, needs, and boundaries. When people feel respected, they are more likely to trust others and feel valued in the relationship.

6. Accountability

Accountability is another essential component of building trust. Accountability means taking responsibility for one's actions, behaviors, and decisions. It involves admitting mistakes, apologizing when necessary, and making amends. When people see someone taking accountability for their actions, they are more likely to trust them because it shows that they are willing to take responsibility for their mistakes and learn from them.

7. Empathy

Empathy is crucial for building trust because it creates a sense of understanding and connection between people. Empathy involves putting oneself in another person's shoes and seeing things from their perspective. It involves listening to others' emotions, feelings, and experiences and responding with kindness and compassion. When people feel understood and heard, they are more likely to trust the other person.

8. Transparency

Transparency is another essential component of building trust. Transparency involves being open and honest about one's intentions, actions, and decisions. It involves sharing information freely and openly, even if it is difficult or uncomfortable. When people feel that someone is transparent, they are more likely to trust them because they know that they are not hiding anything and that they are being upfront and honest.

9. Reliability

Reliability is an essential trait for building trust. Reliability means following through on commitments, showing up on time, and doing what you say you will do. When people can rely on someone to do what they promised, they are more likely to trust them. Reliability also involves being consistent and dependable, which creates a sense of predictability and stability. When people can count on someone to be there for them, they are more likely to trust them.

10. Shared experiences

Shared experiences are a powerful way to build trust among individuals and communities. When people experience something together, they develop a sense of camaraderie and connection. This shared experience can be anything from working on a project together, going on a trip, or simply sharing personal stories. When people have a shared experience, they are more likely to trust each other because they have bonded over something meaningful.

11. Conflict resolution

Conflict is inevitable in any relationship or community. However, how people handle conflict can either strengthen or weaken trust. Effective conflict resolution involves listening to each other's perspectives, finding common ground, and working together to find a solution that everyone can agree on. When people see that someone is willing to work through conflict in a constructive and respectful way, they are more likely to trust them.

Mutual respect is crucial for building trust among individuals and communities. Mutual respect means treating each other as equals, regardless of differences in status, power, or background. It involves recognizing each other's strengths and weaknesses and valuing each other's contributions. When people feel respected by others, they are more likely to trust them.

Conclusion

Building trust takes time, effort, and patience. It requires a combination of communication, consistency, integrity, vulnerability, respect, accountability, empathy, transparency, reliability, shared experiences, conflict resolution, and mutual respect. When people take the time to build trust in their relationships and communities, they create a foundation for cooperation, collaboration, and success. By prioritizing trust, individuals and communities can create strong bonds that can withstand the test of time.

Introduction

Non-violence has been a powerful force throughout history, from Mahatma Gandhi's leadership of India's struggle for independence from British colonialism to the Civil Rights Movement in the United States. Non-violence is not simply the absence of violence but a philosophy that promotes positive change through peaceful means. This article examines the power of non-violence in promoting peace and social change.

What is Non-Violence?

Non-violence is the practice of promoting positive social change through peaceful means. This philosophy can take many forms, including protests, boycotts, strikes, and civil disobedience. The key to non-violence is the absence of physical or emotional harm to others, which distinguishes it from other forms of protest.

Non-violent protests often rely on the principle of moral authority, which means that the protesters' message is more compelling because it is based on moral or ethical principles rather than on coercion or violence. This moral authority can be especially effective in situations where the oppressors have lost the moral high ground, such as in cases of unjust laws or policies.

The Role of Non-Violence in Promoting Peace

Non-violence has been a powerful force for promoting peace throughout history. One of the most prominent examples of this is Mahatma Gandhi's leadership of India's struggle for independence from British colonialism. Gandhi's philosophy of non-violence, or satyagraha, promoted peaceful resistance to British rule through civil disobedience, strikes, and boycotts.

Through his leadership, Gandhi was able to mobilize millions of Indians to peacefully resist British rule, even in the face of violence from British authorities. Gandhi's non-violent resistance was so effective that the British were eventually forced to grant India independence in 1947.

Non-violence has also played a key role in promoting peace in other parts of the world. For example, the Civil Rights Movement in the United States relied on non-violent protests to bring attention to the unjust treatment of African Americans. Leaders such as Martin Luther King Jr. and Rosa Parks used non-violent resistance to promote change and challenge discriminatory laws and policies.

Non-violence has also been used in many other countries to promote peace and social change, including in South Africa during apartheid, in Burma during the 1988 Uprising, and in the Philippines during the People Power Revolution.

The Power of Non-Violence in Social Change

Non-violence can be a powerful tool for promoting social change because it allows marginalized communities to challenge unjust laws and policies without resorting to violence. Non-violent protests can be used to draw attention to social issues, increase public awareness, and put pressure on decision-makers to enact change.

One of the key advantages of non-violent protests is that they can be sustained over long periods of time. This is because non-violent protests rely on moral authority rather than coercion or violence. As a result, non-violent protesters can continue their protests even in the face of opposition or violence from authorities, which can make it difficult for the authorities to maintain their legitimacy.

Non-violent protests can also be used to build solidarity among marginalized communities. By bringing together people from different backgrounds and experiences, non-violent protests can create a sense of unity and common purpose that can be difficult to achieve through other means.

One of the most powerful examples of the power of non-violence in social change is the Civil Rights Movement in the United States. Through their non-violent protests, Civil Rights leaders were able to draw attention to the unjust treatment of African Americans and put pressure on decision-makers to enact change. The Civil Rights Act of 1964 and the Voting Rights Act of 1965 are two examples of the significant changes that were achieved through non-violent protests.

Non-violence can also be a powerful tool for promoting change in other parts of the world. In the Philippines, the People Power Revolution of 1986 used non-violent protests to bring down the authoritarian regime of President Ferdinand Marcos. The protesters relied on peaceful demonstrations, strikes, and civil disobedience to challenge the regime's legitimacy and force Marcos to flee the country.

Similarly, the Velvet Revolution in Czechoslovakia in 1989 used non-violent protests to overthrow the communist government. The protesters used peaceful demonstrations, sit-ins, and strikes to challenge the government's legitimacy and force it to step down.

Non-violent protests can also be effective in promoting change at the local level. In India, the Chipko movement was a non-violent environmental movement that began in the 1970s. The movement aimed to protect forests from deforestation by hugging trees and forming human circles around them. The movement was successful in drawing attention to the issue of deforestation and led to changes in government policy to protect forests.

The Challenges of Non-Violence

While non-violence can be a powerful tool for promoting peace and social change, it is not without its challenges. Non-violent protests can be met with violence from authorities, which can put protesters at risk of injury or death. This was the case during the Civil Rights Movement in the United States, where protesters were met with violence from police and white supremacists.

Non-violent protests can also be difficult to sustain over long periods of time. Protesters may become discouraged or lose momentum, which can make it difficult to achieve meaningful change. Additionally, non-violent protests may not be effective in situations where the oppressors are unwilling to negotiate or compromise.

Conclusion

Non-violence has been a powerful force for promoting peace and social change throughout history. Non-violent protests can be used to draw attention to social issues, increase public awareness, and put pressure on decision-makers to enact change. Non-violence can also be a powerful tool for promoting change at the local level.

However, non-violent protests are not without their challenges. Non-violent protests can be met with violence from authorities, and they can be difficult to sustain over long periods of time. Despite these challenges, non-violence remains an important tool for promoting peace and social change, and it continues to inspire activists around the world today.

Introduction

The world today is facing numerous challenges, from conflict and war to poverty and inequality. These issues have a significant impact on our societies, economies, and the environment. In such times, it is crucial to focus on promoting peace and harmony among individuals and communities. One way to achieve this is by creating a culture of peace, which emphasizes the importance of peaceful conflict resolution, tolerance, and respect for diversity. In this article, we will discuss the importance of promoting a culture of peace in society and explore some ways to create a peaceful culture.

Understanding the Culture of Peace

The United Nations (UN) defines the culture of peace as a "set of values, attitudes, modes of behavior, and ways of life that reject violence and prevent conflicts by tackling their root causes to solve problems through dialogue and negotiation among individuals, groups, and nations." Essentially, the culture of peace aims to promote peaceful coexistence and conflict resolution, as well as tolerance, respect, and understanding among different cultures and religions.

Creating a Culture of Peace

Creating a culture of peace is not a one-time event, but a continuous process that requires the participation of individuals, communities, and governments. Here are some ways to promote a culture of peace:

1. Education

Education is an essential tool for promoting a culture of peace. Educational institutions play a crucial role in shaping individuals' attitudes and beliefs, and promoting values such as respect, tolerance, and peaceful conflict resolution. By incorporating peace education into the curriculum, students can learn about different cultures, religions, and ways of life, as well as how to communicate and solve conflicts peacefully. Additionally, educators can provide practical tools for conflict resolution, such as mediation and negotiation.

2. Dialogue

Dialogue is a critical component of creating a culture of peace. Dialogue allows individuals from different backgrounds to engage in constructive conversations, share ideas, and understand each other's perspectives. Through dialogue, individuals can learn to respect and appreciate diversity and find common ground to resolve conflicts peacefully. Dialogue can occur at different levels, from individuals and communities to national and international levels.

3. Inclusivity

Inclusivity means ensuring that everyone is included and has equal opportunities to participate in society. Inclusive societies are more likely to promote peaceful coexistence and conflict resolution, as individuals feel valued and respected. Promoting inclusivity requires addressing issues such as discrimination, inequality, and marginalization.

Governments can implement policies to promote inclusivity, such as affirmative action and anti-discrimination laws. Additionally, communities can promote inclusivity by creating safe spaces for marginalized groups and encouraging diversity and inclusivity in their organizations and institutions.

4. Empathy

Empathy is the ability to understand and share another person's feelings and experiences. Empathy is a crucial component of creating a culture of peace, as it helps individuals understand and appreciate different perspectives and experiences. By practicing empathy, individuals can overcome stereotypes and prejudices and build more meaningful relationships with people from different backgrounds. Empathy can be promoted through activities such as storytelling, cultural exchange programs, and volunteering.

5. Non-Violent Conflict Resolution

Conflict is inevitable in any society, but it is essential to resolve conflicts peacefully to promote a culture of peace. Non-violent conflict resolution emphasizes the use of peaceful methods, such as mediation and negotiation, to resolve conflicts. Governments can promote non-violent conflict resolution by providing resources for mediation and negotiation and promoting dialogue between conflicting parties. Additionally, communities can create conflict resolution mechanisms, such as community courts, to resolve conflicts peacefully.

Human rights are fundamental rights that every individual is entitled to, regardless of their background or beliefs. Promoting human rights is crucial for creating a culture of peace, as it ensures that individuals are treated with dignity and respect and can live without fear of persecution or discrimination. Governments can promote human rights by implementing policies that protect the rights of all individuals, such as anti-discrimination laws and protecting freedom of expression and religion. Additionally, communities can promote human rights by creating awareness campaigns and advocating for the rights of marginalized groups.

7. Media

The media has a significant influence on shaping public opinion and attitudes towards different issues. By promoting positive messages of peace and non-violence, the media can play a crucial role in creating a culture of peace. Additionally, the media can provide a platform for individuals from different backgrounds to share their stories and experiences, promoting empathy and understanding. Governments can regulate the media to promote positive messages of peace and non-violence, while communities can create their own media platforms to promote positive messages of peace.

8. Interfaith Dialogue

Interfaith dialogue is a crucial component of promoting a culture of peace, as it allows individuals from different religious backgrounds to engage in constructive conversations and learn from each other. Interfaith dialogue promotes respect and tolerance for different religious beliefs, reducing the likelihood of religious conflicts. Interfaith dialogue can occur at different levels, from individual to community and national levels.

Benefits of Promoting a Culture of Peace

Promoting a culture of peace has numerous benefits, including:

1. Reduced violence and conflict

Promoting a culture of peace reduces violence and conflict, as individuals and communities learn to resolve conflicts peacefully. This leads to safer and more stable societies.

2. Improved relationships

Promoting a culture of peace improves relationships among individuals and communities, as it promotes empathy, understanding, and respect for diversity. This leads to more meaningful and positive relationships.

3. Better mental health

Promoting a culture of peace improves mental health, as individuals feel safer, more valued, and less stressed. This leads to improved mental well-being.

4. Economic benefits

Promoting a culture of peace has economic benefits, as it leads to more stable and prosperous societies. This leads to improved living standards and economic growth.

Conclusion

Promoting a culture of peace is essential for creating a safer, more stable, and prosperous world. Creating a culture of peace requires the participation of individuals, communities, and governments and involves promoting values such as respect, tolerance, and peaceful conflict resolution. By promoting a culture of peace, we can reduce violence and conflict, improve relationships, promote better mental health, and realize economic benefits.

Chapter 16. Overcoming Challenges
Identifying the challenges that arise when working towards
peace and offering solutions for overcoming them

Introduction

The pursuit of peace is a noble goal that requires a great deal of effort, patience, and resilience. Unfortunately, there are numerous challenges that arise when working towards peace, and these obstacles can make the journey towards peace seem insurmountable. However, with the right strategies and approaches, it is possible to overcome these challenges and make significant progress towards a more peaceful world. In this article, we will identify some of the key challenges that arise when working towards peace and offer solutions for overcoming them.

Challenges

1. Lack of trust

One of the primary challenges that arise when working towards peace is a lack of trust between parties. This lack of trust can arise from historical conflicts, cultural differences, or other factors, and it can be difficult to overcome. Without trust, it is challenging to establish open communication, negotiate in good faith, or work towards common goals.

2. Power imbalances

Another significant challenge that arises when working towards peace is power imbalances between parties. These imbalances can arise from economic, political, or social factors, and they can create significant obstacles to the negotiation and implementation of peace agreements. Parties with more power may be unwilling to compromise, while those with less power may feel pressured to agree to terms that are not in their best interests.

3. Violence and conflict

Violence and conflict are significant challenges that arise when working towards peace. Ongoing violence can make negotiations and peacebuilding efforts nearly impossible, while the aftermath of violent conflicts can leave deep scars that make it difficult for parties to trust each other and work together towards peace.

4. Cultural differences

Cultural differences can also create significant challenges when working towards peace. These differences can manifest in language barriers, different communication styles, and different values and beliefs. Without understanding and respect for these differences, it can be challenging to establish trust and communicate effectively.

Solutions

1. Building trust

Building trust is a crucial first step in overcoming the challenges that arise when working towards peace. To build trust, it is essential to establish open communication and create opportunities for parties to get to know each other on a personal level. This can be done through social events, cultural exchanges, and other activities that foster mutual understanding and respect.

2. Addressing power imbalances

Addressing power imbalances is another critical step in overcoming the challenges of working towards peace. This can be done by providing support to parties with less power, such as financial assistance, technical support, or political backing. It can also involve creating opportunities for dialogue and negotiation that are fair and equitable, so all parties feel heard and respected.

3. Addressing violence and conflict

Addressing violence and conflict is a significant challenge, but it is essential for making progress towards peace. This can involve mediation efforts, peacekeeping operations, or other forms of intervention that aim to de-escalate tensions and create a safe environment for negotiations to take place. It is also important to address the root causes of violence and conflict, such as economic inequality, political corruption, or cultural tensions.

4. Bridging cultural differences

Bridging cultural differences is another crucial step in overcoming the challenges of working towards peace. This can involve language classes, cultural training, or other forms of education that help parties understand and respect each other's cultures. It can also involve creating opportunities for cultural exchange, such as food festivals, art exhibits, or music concerts, that celebrate diversity and promote mutual understanding.

Conclusion

Working towards peace is a challenging but necessary task that requires a deep commitment to understanding, trust-building, and conflict resolution. By identifying the challenges that arise when working towards peace and implementing strategies to overcome them, it is possible to make significant progress towards a more peaceful world. Whether it involves addressing power imbalances, building trust, addressing violence and conflict, or bridging cultural differences, all of these solutions require a willingness to listen, learn, and compromise. It is important to remember that the journey towards peace is not an easy one, but it is one that is worth taking.

In addition to these solutions, it is also essential to remember the role of individuals in working towards peace. We all have a responsibility to promote peace in our daily lives, whether it involves resolving conflicts with friends or family, supporting peacebuilding efforts in our communities, or advocating for peaceful solutions at the local or national level.

Finally, it is crucial to recognize that the pursuit of peace is an ongoing process. There will always be new challenges and obstacles to overcome, and it is essential to remain vigilant and adaptable in the face of these challenges. By continuing to work towards peace with determination and dedication, we can create a world that is more just, equitable, and peaceful for all.

The book, "The Path to Peace: Overcoming Corruption, Violence, and Hatred in Our World," delves into the various aspects of peacebuilding and how we can overcome corruption, violence, and hatred in society. The book comprises 16 chapters that cover a range of topics such as defining peace, understanding corruption and violence, promoting forgiveness and empathy, and examining the role of religion and dialogue in peacebuilding. The book also explores different methods for preventing violence, building trust, and creating a culture of peace. Additionally, the book identifies the challenges that arise when working towards peace and offers practical solutions for overcoming them. This book is a must-read for anyone interested in understanding and contributing to the promotion of peace and harmony in our world today.

ABOUT THE AUTHOR

Mr. C. P. Kumar is a retired Scientist 'G' from the National Institute of Hydrology, Roorkee, Uttarakhand, India. With a wealth of experience in his field, he has also been practicing alternative healing therapies for several years. He is skilled in Reiki Healing and Chakra Balancing with Pendulum Dowsing, and offers holistic therapy through Emotional Freedom Technique (EFT) for emotional issues. You can email Mr. Kumar at cpkumar@yahoo.com and also visit his Reiki blog at https://reiki-roorkee.blogspot.com/ for more information.

www.ingramcontent.com/pod-product-compliance
Lightning Source LLC
Chambersburg PA
CBHW061351140726
47997CB00003B/1159